I0820288

ISBN 978-1-4549-6171-0

Library of Congress Control Number: 2025024754

Union Square Kids books may be purchased in bulk for business, educational, or promotional use. For more information, please contact your local bookseller or the Hachette Book Group's Special Markets department at special.markets@hbgusa.com.

Printed in Guangdong, China

Lot #:

2 4 6 8 10 9 7 5 3 1

08/25

unionsquareandco.com

Book design by Clarisse Hassan
Edited by Helen Brown

For every little girl who dreams of soaring high, may you reach and touch your stars.—E.W.

For my brother, James.—A.Q.

5 Minute Genius Stories

SIMONE BILES

Written by Ebony Joy Wilkins

Illustrated by Amanda Quartey

How to use this book

In this book you'll find **ten genius stories** to read, each one just **5 minutes** long.

At the end of each story, explore an informative **"all about"** spread.

Want to learn more? Turn to the back of the book to discover a **timeline of key events**.

WHO IS SIMONE BILES?

Simone Biles is one of the greatest athletes of all time—an inspiring gymnast, fearless advocate, and role model. Experience her journey to greatness through some of her most unforgettable moments.

OWNING HER SUCCESS

2019

Simone's influence extends beyond the arena as she designs "GOAT" leotards to reflect her legacy.

RECORD MOVES

May 2021

Simone lands the Yurchenko double pike at the 2021 United States Classic.

STEPPING BACK TO MOVE FORWARD

July 2021

Simone prioritizes her physical and mental health at the Tokyo Olympics, sparking a global conversation.

THE GREATEST MEDAL OF ALL

July 2022

Simone is honored with the Presidential Medal of Freedom for her outstanding achievements.

COMEBACK OF THE YEAR

May 2024

Simone makes a triumphant return to competition at the United States Classic, showcasing her resilience.

INSPIRING FUTURE ATHLETES

July 2024

Simone becomes part of the most diverse United States Women's Gymnastics Team at the Paris 2024 Olympics.

WHICH 5-MINUTE GENIUS STORY WILL YOU READ TODAY?

A STAR IS FOUND

A Life-Changing Field Trip

It was a bright spring day in Texas. Six-year-old Simone Biles stood in the backyard, watching her older brothers, Ronald II and Adam, bounce high on a trampoline.

Simone had recently moved to north Houston to live with her grandparents.

She loved flipping, twirling, and cartwheeling around her new house—but she had no idea that a field trip would soon change her life.

Her brothers would tell her she was too small to join them on the trampoline. But that didn't stop Simone. Determined, she practiced on her own—flipping into bed,

twirling around furniture,

and cartwheeling through the kitchen.

One day, she even somersaulted right onto the trampoline!

It wasn't long before Simone had the chance to show off her moves away from home on a field trip to *Bannon's Gymnastix* in Houston.

Simone soon found her way to the middle of the floor. She extended her legs straight out in front of her, her hands steady at her sides, just as she had seen the older gymnasts do.

She began to pull herself up to a handstand, using her hands to lift her body off the ground.

Simone then went and performed a backflip! The *Bannon's Gymnastix* coaches were stunned.

They couldn't believe a six-year-old could move like that.

One coach, Veronica Banghart, was especially impressed. She sent a note home with Simone, recommending that she join gymnastics classes.

Simone's grandparents, Ronald and Nellie Biles, were surprised at first—but it all made sense. After all, Simone was always flipping and tumbling around the house.

Simone quickly felt at home at *Bannon's*, where she began training twice a week with Coach Aimee, the daughter of Veronica Banghart.

Her talent blossomed. By 2011, Simone was invited to join the *Bannon's* USA Junior Olympic Jet Star team.

A star had been found. Simone was on her way to competing in artistic gymnastics—sparked by one unforgettable field trip.

Artistic GYMNASTICS

The most popular form of gymnastics is artistic gymnastics—that's what Simone competes in. Female gymnasts perform on four apparatuses.

1. Vault

The gymnast runs down a runway, jumps onto a springboard, and pushes off a vaulting table, flipping or twisting in the air before landing.

Springboard

Vaulting table

2. Uneven bars

The gymnast swings, flips, and twists between two horizontal bars set at different heights, showing strength and control.

3. Balance beam

The gymnast performs flips, turns, and dance moves on a narrow beam, using balance and concentration to stay on without falling.

4. Floor

The gymnast performs a series of flips, jumps, and dance moves on a springy floor, showing off strength, grace, and creativity to music.

Nine judges decide a gymnast's score. Each score comes from two parts: **how difficult the routine** is and **how well the gymnast performs it.**

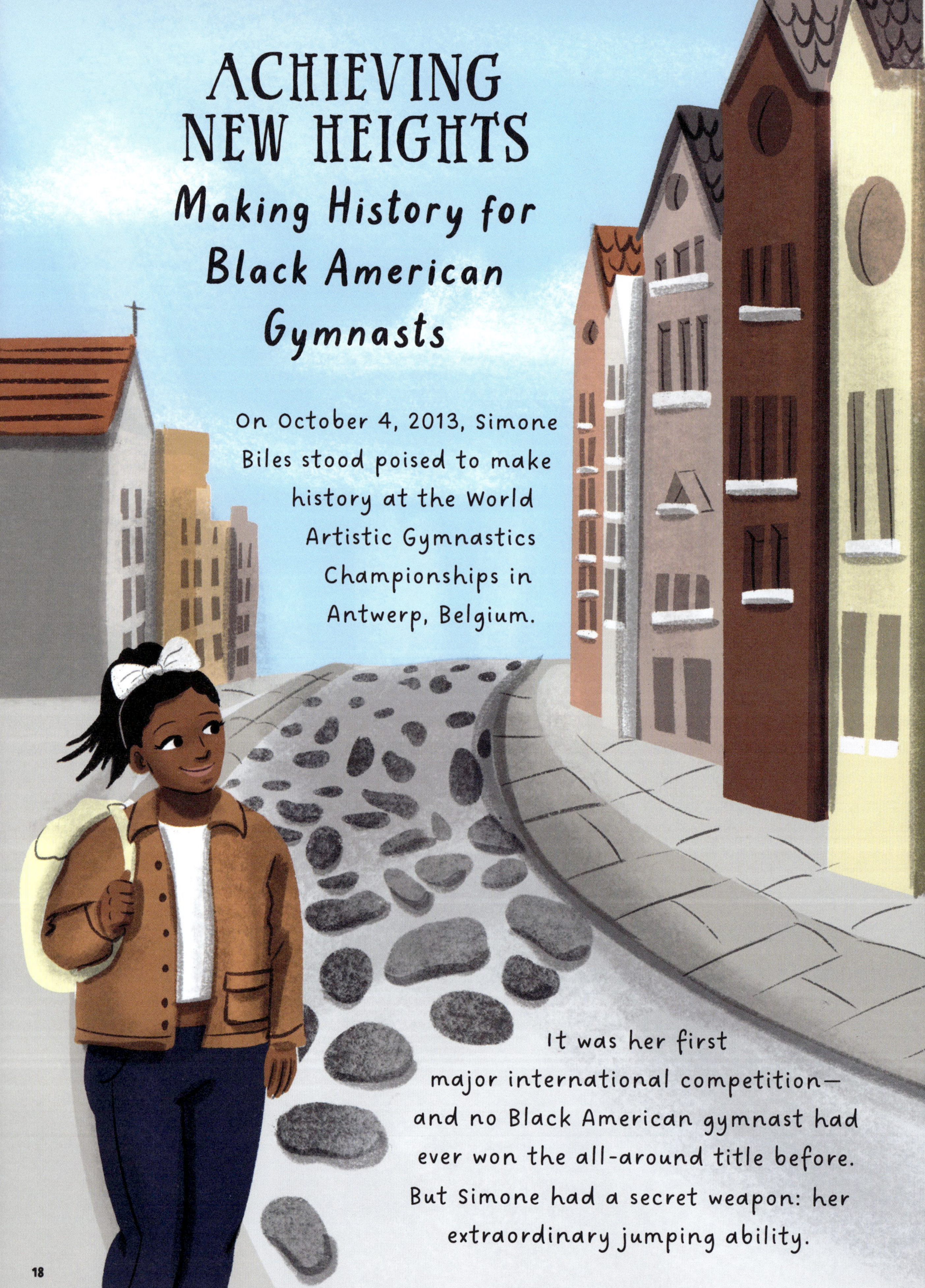

ACHIEVING NEW HEIGHTS

Making History for Black American Gymnasts

On October 4, 2013, Simone Biles stood poised to make history at the World Artistic Gymnastics Championships in Antwerp, Belgium.

It was her first major international competition—and no Black American gymnast had ever won the all-around title before. But Simone had a secret weapon: her extraordinary jumping ability.

She was competing across all four events—vault, uneven bars, balance beam, and floor exercise—with combined scores determining the all-around champion.

From the moment she stepped into the arena, the roar of the crowd threatened to overwhelm her.

But her grandmother's voice echoed in her mind: "Don't go out there to compete against anyone else. Just go out there and be the best Simone you can be."

At sixteen years old, Simone had climbed the ranks to the elite level 10 squad at *Bannon's Gymnastix*. She was now standing on the world stage, ready to take flight.

The Amanar vault was her first test—a difficult move requiring a round-off onto the springboard, a back handspring onto the vault, and two-and-a-half twists before landing. Simone stuck it with precision, drawing gasps from the audience.

The uneven bars came next.

She performed a piked Tkatchev flawlessly,

followed by a Pak salto

and a breathtaking full-twisting double back dismount.

Her balance beam routine combined artistry and athleticism, and each move was met with thunderous applause.

But it was her floor routine that brought the crowd to its feet.

Her incredible jumping ability allowed her to pack more difficulty into her routine—and land it all with confidence.

When the scores came in, Simone had earned 60.216 points, claiming the all-around title—and making history as the first Black American gymnast to ever do so.

"I just had to believe in myself," she said, reflecting years later in an interview with *Vanity Fair*. And she did. Her belief—and her jumping—carried her even further.

In the days that followed, she added a gold medal on floor, silver on vault, and bronze on beam.

As Simone went home with her grandmother,
she thought about everything that had happened.

Her extraordinary height in the air had earned her not just bonus points, but a place in the record books. She didn't just leap in competition—she soared into history.

How HIGH can Simone JUMP?

Simone is 4 feet 8 inches tall, but she can reach more than twice her own height during the peak of her routines.

Simone builds up **momentum** and **kinetic energy** during her tumbling run, which she releases when she pushes off the ground with her powerful leg muscles. This allows her to perform more complex moves while in the air.

Competitive gymnastics floors are specially designed with **springs** that make the surface safer for landing and give athletes like Simone extra height on tumbles.

Simone's **strength-to-weight ratio** allows her to jump so high while keeping her body straight.

Simone's routines often showcase her incredible jumps, especially during her **Yurchenko double pike vault**, where she soars 12 feet into the air.

Simone's jumping height in gymnastics is important because it allows her to perform **high-difficulty skills across all apparatus**, setting her apart from other gymnasts.

LANDING "THE BILES"

Winning Her First Olympic Gold

In August 2016, under the bright lights of Rio de Janeiro's Olympic arena, the Games were in full swing. Nineteen-year-old Simone, already a rising star at the World Championships, was ready to debut on the sport's grandest stage.

Competing with the United States women's gymnastics team—known as the "Final Five"—against fierce rivals from Russia, China, and Great Britain, Simone was chasing her first Olympic gold.

She had already dazzled the judges with a stunning score of 15.433 on the balance beam. And she knew just the move she would need to do on the floor to secure gold.

The arena in Brazil buzzed with anticipation. Dressed in a sparkling red, white, and blue leotard, Simone raised her arms high, tuning out the deafening cheers of fans chanting, "Let's go, Simone!"

As a vibrant Latin medley filled the arena, Simone launched into motion, combining strength and elegance in every step.

Each movement was exact—her leaps, flips, and jumps executed with flawless precision.

The crowd watched in awe as she flew across the floor.

Then came *the* moment.
It was time for "The Biles."

This move—first debuted by Simone at the 2013 World Championships—was now being performed on the Olympic stage for the first time.

Simone soared into the air, twisting mid-flight in a double layout with a half-twist. The crowd held its breath.

When she stuck the landing, the stadium erupted. She didn't need to see the scoreboard to know: she had nailed it.

Then the score flashed on the screen—a near-perfect 15.800.

She turned to find her family in the crowd. Her grandparents and her sister Adria were on their feet, cheering.

Her teammates—Gabby Douglas, Laurie Hernandez, Madison Kocian, Aly Raisman—stood united, hands raised in celebration.

Simone had landed her signature move on the world's biggest stage—and with it, achieved her first individual Olympic gold.

She came to the Rio Olympics a rising star.

She left a legend.

The "BILES"

"The Biles" is a groundbreaking gymnastics move first performed by Simone Biles during a floor routine. It features a double layout with a half twist.

1.
Simone starts by **running fast** across the mat.

2.
At the end of her run, she **jumps forwards** and up into the air.

3.
Once in the air, Simone keeps her body straight. This is called a **layout position.**

4.
She then does her first **backflip.**

5.

before flipping again, this time turning her body sideways in the air. This is a **half twist.**

6.

As she comes down, Simone looks for the ground to make sure her feet will land. This is called **spotting.**

7.

As she lands, her arms go up high. This helps her to **balance** and not fall over.

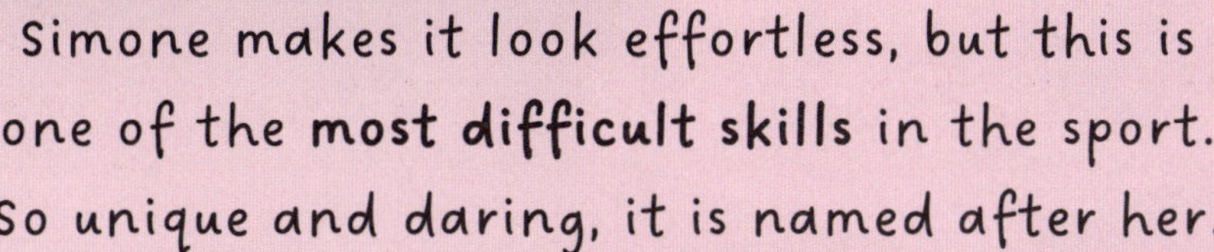

Simone makes it look effortless, but this is one of the **most difficult skills** in the sport. So unique and daring, it is named after her.

THE "GOAT" STATUS

Becoming the Greatest of All Time

By the 1990s, the term "GOAT" came to stand for "Greatest of All Time"—a title reserved for athletes with unmatched skill, determination, and resilience. Simone Biles was on her way to earning that title through all three.

Coach Aimee Boorman, recognizing the fire in Simone's eyes, crafted a training plan that pushed Simone to the limit.

Days turned into weeks, weeks into months, as Simone practiced, trying to perfect each move.

Ahead lay the 2019 World Artistic Gymnastics Championships in Stuttgart, Germany—a global stage where she could shine.

By then, Simone had become America's "golden girl," with fans expecting nothing short of perfection. But behind her confident smile were complex emotions.

Simone focused on building mental resilience, working with experts to help her manage the pressure to be perfect.

In a March 2016 interview with *Time* magazine, she reflected, "Something that has helped me in dealing with that pressure is remembering that gymnastics is just one part of my life."

That mindset became her anchor. And so, when Simone stepped onto the competition floor in Stuttgart in October 2019, she was both mentally and physically prepared.

She began with her floor routine—turning, twisting, jumping, and dancing to the rhythm. But with so much power behind her runs, she stepped out of bounds . . . twice.

Simone noticed her mistakes immediately. Still, she pushed forward, her determination stronger than ever.

Then came the defining moment: the Biles II.
A triple-double move so risky, it could make or break her.
But Simone had invented this move. She knew what to do.

Taking a deep breath, she launched into the air, twisting and flipping with precision. A hush swept through the crowd—and then it erupted as she landed solidly, almost effortlessly.

Simone had done it. Her victory was not just about skill—it was about mental determination and resilience, too.

From that moment on, the world began calling her the GOAT of gymnastics—the Greatest of All Time.

The "GOAT"

Simone is considered by many people to be the "GOAT"—the Greatest of All Time—because she is the best in her sport.

MEDALS

Simone has won the most **Olympic and World Championship medals** of any gymnast, male or female. She has also won the most national titles of any American gymnast.

Simone has more than 40 medals in total!

CONSISTENCY

In 2013, she won every **all-around competition** she entered and kept the streak going for more than a decade.

DIFFICULTY

Simone performs skills that most gymnasts don't even attempt, and some are even named after her in the official **Code of Points**—the rulebook that defines gymnastics scoring at all competition levels.

The Biles (balance beam) has a **D-score of 6.0 points**, making it the most difficult start value for the balance beam.

LEADERSHIP

She is honest with her teammates about her **feelings**, which helps build trust and confidence with the team.

INSPIRING THE NEXT GENERATION

She is a **role model** for young athletes, and continuously pushes the sport to be better, safer, and more fun.

OWNING HER SUCCESS

Designing Her "GOAT" Leotard

By 2019, Simone had won twenty-five medals at world championships and five at the Olympic Games in Rio. She had truly earned her title of the GOAT—the Greatest of All Time.

Simone was incredibly proud of everything that she had achieved, and she wanted to be able to express this to the world. But she wanted to do more than just show her medals.

Simone thought about how she could express her individuality while she was competing, and an idea came to her.

She decided to design her very own leotard—one that boldly featured a symbol now attached to her legacy. A dazzling rhinestone goat for the GOAT.

For years, gymnastics had been a sport where athletes often wore similar uniforms.

And one where standing out too boldly could sometimes be seen as poor sportsmanship or disrespectful to tradition.

Simone decided to change that.

Through her designs—including high-neck cuts, angled sleeves, and even a striking snakeskin pattern—she embraced personal expression.

And no leotard is more individual than one with a crystal-encrusted goat head on it.

It was a bold move that made some old-school fans uncomfortable.

But Simone wasn't fazed.

"[The haters] were joking like, 'I swear, if she put a goat on her leo[tard], blah, blah, blah.' That would make them so angry. And then I was like, 'Oh, that's actually a good idea.' And so that's exactly what we did."

By doing so, Simone represented to others—especially the next generation—a woman in sports speaking her truth and owning it.

There was no shame to be felt in being the best.

"I hope that kids growing up watching this don't or aren't ashamed of being good at whatever they do," she said in a 2021 interview with *Marie Claire*.

Simone's leotards were a powerful message to inspire others to embrace their greatness.

Designing her own LEOTARDS

Simone designed some of her own leotards and made them symbolic of her achievements.

Simone first revealed her "**GOAT**" **leotard** design in 2019 during training ahead of the U.S. Gymnastics Championships.

She later incorporated the goat motif into her competition leotards.

Some of Simone's leotards have stars and patterns that look like the **American flag**, showing support for her country.

For the Paris 2024 Olympics, Simone helped design leotards for the entire team, featuring **6,359 shiny crystals** inspired by French fashion and art.

It took **two years** to design and produce the leotards worn by the United States gymnastics team at the 2024 Olympics.

RECORD MOVES

Landing the Yurchenko Double Pike

At twenty-four years old, Simone Biles was preparing for the 2021 United States Classic, and anticipation was high.

Everyone knew she was chasing something historic: the Yurchenko double pike, one of the most difficult vaults in gymnastics.

If she landed it, she would become the first woman ever to do so in competition.

"This vault is definitely the most difficult to do, because it's just very precise so that you can land it," Simone later explained in an interview with *Vanity Fair*.

Each practice session was a battle.

She would run up to the vault, plant her feet, spring into the air.

But time and again, she'd bend her body too much . . .

Or bend it too little.

The mat absorbed her falls, but the frustration was heavy.

Her coaches offered words of encouragement, reminding her of her potential on the vault.

With the Tokyo Olympics looming, the pressure mounted—but so did Simone's determination.

So she kept practicing, and kept believing in herself.

By May 22, 2021, she was ready.

At the United States Classic, Simone stood on the runway, heart pounding. She took a deep breath, focused on her technique, and sprinted toward the vault.

The crowd watched as she soared into the air, her body twisting and turning with complete control.

For a moment, it seemed as if time had stopped.

Then, she landed, perfectly.
The crowd erupted in cheers.

Simone had landed the Yurchenko double pike at a competition and etched her name in the record books.

The YURCHENKO double pike

In 2021, Simone became the first woman ever to land a Yurchenko double pike in competition.

It is considered the most difficult vault in women's gymnastics. It's so difficult that few male gymnasts have tried it.

Run up

Hands go down on the mat

A round-off onto the springboard

A back hand-spring onto the vaulting table

This move is an evolution of a "Yurchenko", a vault skill invented by the Russian gymnast **Natalia Yurchenko** in 1982.

First flip

Second flip

Simone scored **16.1**, which is higher than either of her gold medal-winning vaults at the 2016 Rio Olympics.

Since the 2016 Rio Olympics, the Yurchenko double pike has carried a **lower score** to reduce the incentive to attempt this dangerous vault.

Land with both feet on the mat

Simone nailed the move wearing a white leotard with a sparkly **rhinestone goat**. It was a nod to her status as the Greatest of all Time.

In a gymnastics competition, each gymnast wears a **number** on their back so the judges know who they are!

STEPPING BACK TO MOVE FORWARD

Prioritizing Mental Health

At the 2021 Tokyo Olympics, 24-year-old Simone Biles was at the top of her game. But she showed the world that being an athlete doesn't just mean being physically strong, it means being mentally strong as well.

When Simone stepped onto the vault runway, she was feeling pressure to keep up her winning streak.

She planned to perform a 2½-twisting vault.

She sprinted forward, launched into the air, and twisted gracefully—but mid-air, something went wrong.

Suddenly, she felt dizzy, so dizzy that she seemed to be disconnected from her body.

Though she tried her best to stay focused, her mind stalled after just 1½ twists,

and before she knew it, she had overshot her landing. She bent her knees and waved her arms wildly to catch her balance.

Gasps rippled through the arena. What had just happened to the greatest gymnast of all time?

It was the "twisties," a dangerous mental block that gymnasts dread.

Simone stood, clutching her knees, her face a mask of confusion and frustration. It wasn't pain in her body—it was her mind.

She walked to the sidelines and spoke quietly with her coach, Cecile Landi.

Moments later, the announcement came: Simone would withdraw.

"I have to focus on my mental health . . . We have to protect our minds and our bodies and not just go out and do what the world wants us to do," Simone said to sports journalists.

Simone wasn't just competing for medals—she was carrying the weight of a nation, her teammates, fans across the globe, and the expectations that come with being the greatest gymnast of all time. It had taken its toll.

"It was hard," she admitted a few months later during an interview on NBC's *Today* show.

"To do something that I've done forever and just not be able to do it because of everything I've gone through is really crazy because I love this sport so much," she said.

!!!

We support you!!

Go Simone

The best role model

Simone feared people would be unkind, but instead, she received an outpouring of support from many for prioritizing her mental health.

After Tokyo, Simone took two years to rest. And in doing so, she reminded everyone: true strength lies in knowing when to step back.

By putting her mental health and well-being first, Simone Biles redefined what it meant to be a champion.

The BRAIN and BODY must work in unison

When a gymnast's brain and body stop working together they might experience "the twisties." It's as if the brain loses track of the body's position in the air, making it difficult—and sometimes frightening—to regain control and land safely.

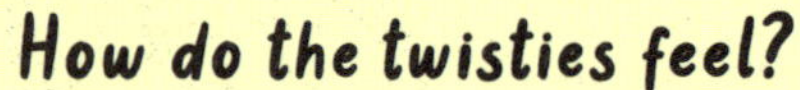

How do the twisties feel?

Imagine spinning super-fast on a swing and suddenly not knowing which way is up or down—that's kind of what the twisties feel like for gymnasts.

The twisties can happen because:

Gymnasts feel **nervous** or **stressed**.

Their **brain is too tired to focus.**

They are trying **new, hard tricks.**

Gymnasts can overcome the twisties by:

Taking breaks: Resting helps the brain reset.

Focusing on a different skill: Doing easier moves helps a gymnast get their rhythm back . . . and their confidence.

Seeking help: Coaches can help with tips and encouragement.

Simone's choice to stop competing was a big deal. It paved the way for other athletes to **express their feelings** in high-pressure situations.

THE GREATEST MEDAL OF ALL

Receiving the Presidential Medal of Freedom

By 2022, Simone Biles had become the most decorated gymnast in history, with an astonishing thirty-two Olympic and World Championship medals.

But on July 7 of that year, she was about to receive something even more meaningful: the Presidential Medal of Freedom—the highest civilian honor in the United States.

Wearing a black dress, Simone walked into the East Room of the White House, her trademark smile lighting up the room.

She took her seat among the other honorees, sitting in the same row as fellow Olympian and soccer player Megan Rapinoe.

President Joe Biden stepped up to the podium to recognize their contributions.

When it was Simone's turn, he welcomed her with a warm smile and a gentle pat on the back.

As they stood together, her accomplishments were read aloud by the military aide:

"Simone Biles is an inspiring symbol of strength, grace, and pride in those three letters: USA."

The military aide called Simone a "once-in-a-generation athlete," and said there were many moments that had defined Simone along her journey to athletic greatness.

Her courage off the mat was equally praised. The military aide honored Simone for speaking openly about mental health, saying she "speak[s] up for justice and the wellness of body and mind."

President Biden placed the medal around her neck and later shared on social media:

"When we see Simone compete, we're witnessing unmatched power and grace. [She] represents the best of America."

With the Presidential Medal of Freedom gleaming around her neck, Simone wasn't just a superstar gymnast, she was a symbol of excellence to her country.

What is the PRESIDENTIAL MEDAL OF FREEDOM?

The Presidential Medal of Freedom is awarded by the President of the United States to people who have made incredible contributions to America.

13 gold stars on a blue background represents the Great Seal of the United States, a unique symbol of America's national identity.

Five gold bald eagles surround the star. The bald eagle is the national bird of America; it first appeared on the national seal in 1782.

Red, white, and blue are the colors of the American flag.

Other legendary athletes who have received the Presidential Medal of Freedom include Jackie Robinson (1984), Muhammad Ali (2005), Billie Jean King (2009), and Michael Jordan (2016). **Simone was the youngest, receiving it at 25 years old!**

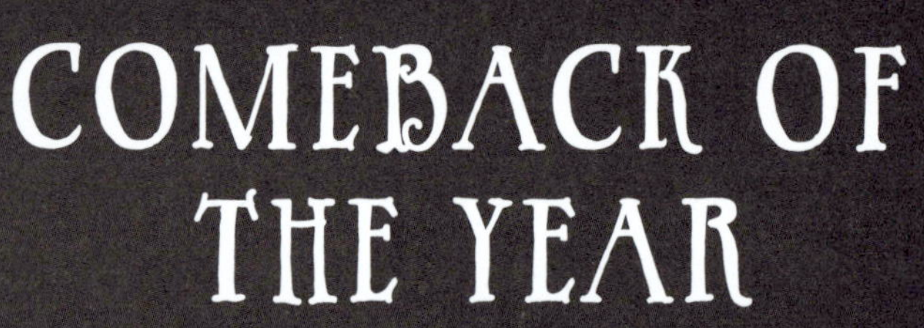

COMEBACK OF THE YEAR

A Triumphant Return

In 2021, Simone Biles stunned the world when she withdrew from the Tokyo Olympics due to the "twisties," a dangerous mental block.

At 24, she chose her mental health over medals.

Three years later, on May 18, 2024, Simone was in Hartford, Connecticut, marking the start of her season before the next Olympics.

Over the months leading up to it, she had rebuilt herself—mentally and physically.

She balanced training with joyful moments spent with loved ones. She returned to her sport not only stronger, but wiser.

Now, standing at the United States Classic, she was competing to earn a spot on Team USA for the Paris 2024 Olympics.

Walking to each apparatus—vault, beam, uneven bars, and floor—Simone radiated grace.

On the beam, she began with a shaky landing but quickly regained balance, delivering a stunning sequence of triple spins, backflips, and a twist-filled dismount that had the crowd on their feet.

Her floor routine dazzled, blending electrifying flips with elegant choreography.

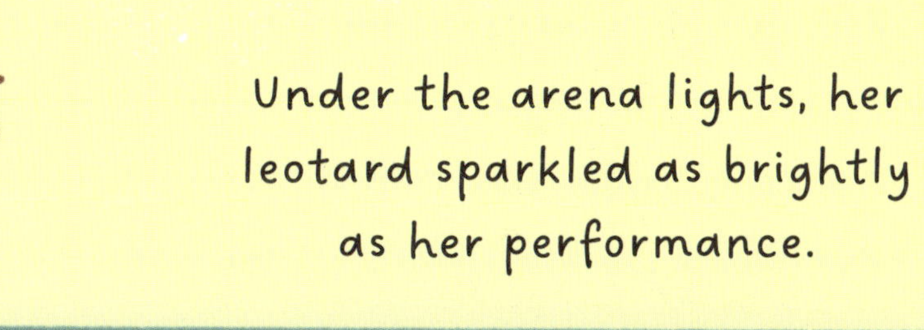

Under the arena lights, her leotard sparkled as brightly as her performance.

When the final scores flashed, Simone's all-around score of 59.500 placed her far ahead of her competition.

59.500

"I was just happy to be back out there. Get through those nerves again, feel that adrenaline," she later told reporters.

Simone's comeback was a success. The 2024 Paris Olympics were hers for the taking.

The LAUREUS WORLD COMEBACK OF THE YEAR award

Simone won the 2024 Laureus World Comeback of the Year award for her return to gymnastics after a two-year break.

The comeback award celebrates athletes who have **overcome major challenges**, such as injuries or personal issues, to make a successful return to their sport.

"Her journey from an Olympic exit . . . to a triumphant comeback, has been as inspirational as anything Biles has done in competition," the academy said about Simone.

The prestigious awards are sometimes called **the "Oscars" of sports.**

Serena Williams won the Laureus World Comeback of the Year in 2007.

Lewis Hamilton won the Laureus World Sportsman of the Year in 2020—a joint win with **Lionel Messi.**

The trophy is designed to represent the **human form** in motion.

Simone previously received the **Laureus Sportswoman of the Year award** in 2017, 2019, and 2020.

INSPIRING FUTURE ATHLETES

Part of the Most Diverse United States Women's Gymnastics Team

It was July 2024, and the Paris Olympics were in full swing. Inside the buzzing Bercy Arena on Tuesday 30, 27-year-old Simone Biles stood amid roaring crowds of fans, families, and fellow athletes.

She was part of a historic moment—the most diverse United States women's gymnastics team ever assembled.

Growing up, Simone didn't have anyone who looked like her in the sport she loved.

"I know what it's like being the only Black girl on the team, and not having a role model," Simone shared in 2024 in her Netflix documentary, *Simone Biles Rising*.

But today, Simone was part of the most diverse gymnastics team in United States history, with four of the five gymnasts being women of color. Alongside Simone, the team included:

Jordan Chiles,
whose power and charisma lit up the floor

Jade Carey,
a vault and floor specialist driven by unshakable determination

Together they were set to represent the United States in the women's artistic gymnastics team all-around event.

Earlier that day, Jordan called for a team huddle. Sitting cross-legged on the floor, the gymnasts opened up—sharing fears, hopes, and insecurities.

Suni spoke about the pressure of living up to her Olympic title.

Hezly, the youngest,
admitted she was nervous
competing alongside legends
she'd grown up admiring.

In that space of honesty,
they found strength in
representation—laughing,
supporting, and promising
to lift one another up.

Later, standing before the press, their connection was undeniable. Simone smiled proudly at the team beside her—a living symbol of how far the sport had come.

For the next generation of gymnasts, the question wasn't whether they belonged.

They knew they did.

You have to SEE IT to BE IT

Simone recognizes the importance of having a role model, someone who represents the person you envision yourself being.

That's why Simone partnered with **Friends of the Children**, bringing the program to her hometown of Houston, Texas.

This initiative pairs foster children with long-term mentors—**"Friends"**—who support them from kindergarten through high school.

Simone was in foster care as a child. She was six years old when her grandparents **adopted** her and her younger sister, Adria.

Her grandparents provided her with the support that allowed her to pursue her gymnastics dreams.

Each May, during **National Foster Care Month,** Simone speaks to the Friends of the Children national network. She encourages them to work hard to achieve their goals.

Simone invites children from the program to **visit her gym** in Spring, Texas. She spends time with them, inspiring them to find their own dreams.

SIMONE BILES'S JOURNEY TO BECOMING A LEGENDARY ATHLETE

Simone Arianne Biles is born in **Columbus, Ohio** on March 14.

Simone discovers gymnastics at age six after a **daycare field trip** to a local gym. Training begins!

Simone makes her elite debut at the **American Classic**.

Simone defends her national all-around title and wins four gold medals (team, all-around, vault, floor) and one bronze (balance beam) at the **Rio Olympics**.

Simone claims four gold medals at **the World Championships**, including all-around, bringing her total to a record 13 World Championship golds—the most of any gymnast, male or female.

Simone wins her sixth national all-around title. At the World Championships, she wins five gold medals, becoming **the most decorated gymnast** (male or female) **in World Championship history**.

After the **Tokyo Olympics** were postponed by a year, Simone withdraws from several events, citing mental health concerns. She later returns to win a bronze medal in the balance beam.

Simone competes at the **Visa Championships** (formerly known as the USA Gymnastics National Championships). She finishes third overall in the junior division.

Simone wins her **first national all-around title** at the senior level at the P&G Gymnastics Championships. Later that year, she claims gold in the floor exercise and captures her first World all-around title at the World Artistic Gymnastics Championships.

Simone wins her second consecutive national all-around title and four gold medals at the **World Championships**, claiming the world titles on beam, floor, and in the all-around.

Simone wins the P&G Gymnastics Championships for the third time in a row and four gold medals at the World Championships. She becomes the **most decorated American woman** in World Championship history at that time.

Simone receives the **Presidential Medal of Freedom**, the nation's highest civilian honor.

Simone returns to competition, winning the United States Classic and her **eighth national all-around title**. She wins four medals at the World Championships, including gold in the team event.

Simone competes at the **Paris Olympics,** where she wins four medals, breaking the record for most Olympic medals won by an American gymnast.